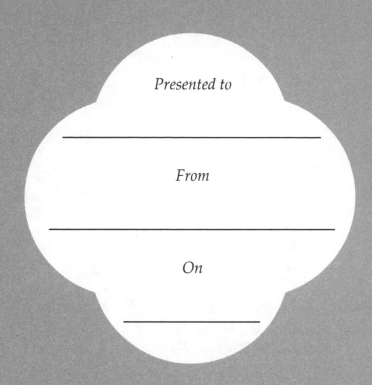

Presented to

_____

From

_____

On

_____

THE CHILDREN'S BIBLE

Volume 1

A Golden Press / Funk & Wagnalls, Inc. Book
Published by Western Publishing Company, Inc.

COPYRIGHT © 1981, 1965 BY WESTERN PUBLISHING COMPANY, INC. COPYRIGHT © 1962 BY FRATELLI FABBRI, MILAN, ALL RIGHTS RESERVED. PRINTED IN THE U.S.A. PUBLISHED BY GOLDEN PRESS, NEW YORK, BY ARRANGEMENT WITH WESTERN PUBLISHING—HACHETTE INTERNATIONAL, S.A., GENEVA. GOLDEN® AND GOLDEN PRESS® are trademarks of Western Publishing Company, Inc.

Distributed by Funk & Wagnalls, Inc., New York

Library of Congress Catalog Card Number: 81-81439

ISBN 0-8343-0038-9 (Volume 1)
ISBN 0-8343-0037-0 (12 Volume Set)

CONTENTS

FOREWORD

No book has influenced the world more than the Bible. These holy scriptures are the foundations of the great Christian and Jewish faiths, and people the world over believe in, and live by, the Bible's teachings.

The Bible is a collection of stories about God's chosen people. Some of the stories are frightening, some are funny, and still others are deeply moving. The Bible is also a history of these people. For Christians and Jews, however, the Bible is something more than literature or history. They believe it is God's word. They believe that God showed himself to men and women in its pages. In the Bible, God tells men and women who he is and what he wants from them.

We read how God created the world out of nothingness, and put men and women, whom he made in his own image, in it to worship him. God gave his people ten great commandments by which to lead their lives. And people everywhere use these commandments to tell right from wrong, and to guide them in their relationships with other people and with God.

The God we read about in the Bible often seems like a person. God enters into friendships with men and women, he talks to them and leads them. Christians believe Jesus Christ is God, which means that they believe God walked among men and women. The Jewish people believe that God had special plans for their nation. They believe that God wanted the patriarch Jacob, whom he renamed Israel, to teach all nations about him. The Bible gives us an account of both these beliefs.

Christians and Jews read the Bible often. They say that they need the Bible the way a baby needs milk: It nourishes them and makes them healthy and strong. They read the Bible in order to know who God is and what he wants them to do.

The Bible recounts the history of the people of Israel. The Old Testament describes the government and the religious faith of the Jewish people, and records the long and hard wars that the people of Israel had to fight against their powerful neighbors. It tells us of the eventual collapse of the Kingdom of Israel and the exile of the people in the year 587 B.C. The New Testament records the life of Jesus and the story of Israel when it was under the power of the Roman Empire.

The word Bible means "the books." The plural is used because the Bible is not really one book but a collection of 66 small books. Each book has a different title, like "Genesis" or "Isaiah"

or "Luke." The books were written and collected by different people over a long period of time. The writers were sometimes people who had actually experienced what they wrote about, sometimes they were disciples of the people they described, and sometimes they simply copied down the stories and history which everyone in the community already knew.

Before the Bible stories were written down in the form we have them today, people heard them told by storytellers. As the people of Israel wandered through the desert or tended their flocks of sheep and goats, they would listen to the stories about their history and about their great leaders and teachers. The stories existed in this form long before they were written down, and were already an important part of the Hebrew heritage.

When the different parts of the Bible were written down for the first time, two languages were used. The Old Testament was written mainly in Hebrew, the New Testament was written in Greek. Christians read both the Old and the New Testaments. They believe that the story of Jesus completes the meaning of the Old Testament. The Jewish people read the Old Testament. In their understanding, God revealed himself completely in the books of the Old Testament.

Christians and Jews have always been eager to translate their book into every language of the world so that all men and women can understand who God is. The Hebrew scriptures were translated into Greek in approximately 285 B.C. and both the Hebrew and the Greek scriptures could be read in Latin by the year 400. The earliest English translation of part of the Bible was made in England in the 7th century and the first complete English Bible was printed in 1535. Today the Bible can be read in almost all the languages spoken on this planet.

The great value which Christians and Jews place on making the Bible available to all people can be seen in the fact that it was the first book printed on the newly invented printing press in 1456.

The *Children's Bible* is designed to bring the exciting world of the Bible to your children in a language they can understand. The stories selected are the ones children love best, and they are presented with rich illustrations on every page to make them easier for young readers to understand. Each volume has its own introduction, which describes the historical and geographical settings of the stories, and an illustrated glossary, which provides helpful definitions and maps. This new edition of the *Children's Bible* will make reading the Bible a family event in your home.

THE
OLD TESTAMENT

INTRODUCTION

The first volume of the *Children's Bible* comes from Genesis, the first book of the Bible. Genesis means "beginning" or "origin." The Book of Genesis tells us the story of two different beginnings. First it recounts the beginning of the human race. It describes how God created the world and then put the first man and woman in the Garden of Eden. It also tells us about the origins of God's chosen people, the Hebrews or Israelites. The history of the Israelites began when God called Abraham to live in the land of Canaan.

Abraham led his people into Canaan from their home in the lands east of Canaan. Abraham and his people were nomads. This means that they had no permanent home, but travelled from place to place, herding their flocks of sheep and goats in search of food and water. Water was very scarce in the land of Canaan. As a result, the people who lived there became skilled at building wells to catch and save the rain. Abraham and his people tried to stay close to these wells.

The life of the nomad was difficult. Nomads were always in search of food for their sheep. As soon as the sheep had eaten all the grass in one place, the nomads moved on to areas of fresh grass. When traveling, they piled their tents and belongings on top of their donkeys. Small children rode high up on the donkey's back while their older sisters and brothers walked alongside. Usually the nomads did not wander far. But when the rain was scarce and the flocks could not find grass, then the people went on long journeys. Abraham led his people as far away as Egypt in search of water and pasture.

When the nomads found a place that was rich in grass and water, they settled down for a short period of time. Then they planted some crops for food, though usually these were crops which they could harvest quickly, since the people knew they would have to soon move again. The whole family worked very hard because there were many chores to do. Someone had to carry water from the well, someone else had to make the clothing and repair the tents, someone else had to watch the sheep and goats.

The job of minding the flocks was often given to girls. Tending the flocks was very difficult. The girls of the tribe had to keep the sheep together and make sure that none wandered off. If one sheep did wander away from the rest, the girls went to look for it. They also had to watch out for the wild animals that roamed near the flocks.

The people lived in tents which were made out of the skin of goats. Nomads usually ate bread, cheese, figs, and olives, and drank goats' milk. On special occasions, such as a great religious holiday, they killed a lamb or a calf and all the people sat down together for a big feast and celebration.

Men and women during the time of Abraham wore short skirts made out of animal skins or long flowing robes made out of linen or wool. They wore their robes loosely in an effort to stay cool in the sun. The people of Canaan were famous for the beautiful dyes they invented, and they dyed their robes many colors. Around their waists they wore leather belts which they used to carry their tools.

The Hebrew people believed that God made animals to help men and women. Many different kinds of animals lived in the land of Canaan. Beautiful and swift deer roamed the countryside. The people used donkeys and mules to help them carry heavy objects and they rode them on their journeys in search of food for their flocks. The Hebrew people learned about horses from the Egyptians, who used them in battle.

There were also many dangerous wild animals in the land. Lions wandered about on the edges of settlements, threatening the lives of people and their flocks. Bears lived in the hills and woods. There were many different kinds of snakes in the land. Most of these were harmless, but there were a large number of very poisonous snakes in Canaan.

The most important animals, of course, were the ones which the farmers and shepherds raised. The Hebrew people in Canaan raised cattle. They made leather for their clothing from the cattle and they made food from the cows' milk. The Hebrew people used oxen to pull their wagons. They also raised sheep and goats for food and clothing. From the sheep's wool, people made their long and flowing robes. Goats were easy to raise, because they could find food for themselves even in the rocks and sand. Cheese was made from the goats' milk.

The Hebrew people of Canaan lived in tribes. The tribes were like big families. All the tribe members were either related to each other or else they all came from the same place. The people of the same tribe called each other brother and sister. The flocks were usually owned by the whole tribe, not by any one of the families that belonged to the tribe. The Hebrew people organized themselves into tribes because desert life was easier if everyone worked together. As a tribe, there were more people around to help with the farming and to protect the flocks.

Whenever an important decision had to be made, the heads of all the families in the tribe gathered together to talk.

After they had discussed the problem, they would choose their course of action. They decided where the tribe would go in search of pasture. The leaders of the tribe in the Book of Genesis were old and wise men called patriarchs. Abraham was the first patriarch of the Hebrew people.

The Hebrew nomads of Canaan were peaceful people and they did everything they could to avoid battle with the other people who lived in Canaan. On occasion, however, they would have trouble with one of their neighbors. When this happened, the heads of the families got together to prepare for war. The members of the tribe protected each other.

At the time of the patriarchs Abraham and Isaac, however, the Hebrew people rarely went to war. They did not fear strangers, but were usually very kind and generous to them. If a traveller whom they did not know wandered into their camp, they treated him with great respect. They offered him water to wash himself and they gave him food to eat. When he left them, they gave him more food to take with him on his journey, and they helped him find his way.

The Hebrew people believed that a single God created the world. They believed that all the good things of nature, such as the birds, the flowers, and sky, and the fish of the sea, were gifts which God gave to men and women. They also said that when God was angry, he showed his anger in the thunder and lightning, and in the hot sun which dried up their water. But they believed that God only became angry when men and women did something wrong. The Hebrew people believed that God created men and women to be his friends and to care for the beautiful world which he made for them.

Wherever they went — in the forests, in the desert, and outside the cities — the Hebrew people of Canaan set up altars so they could pray to their God. They burned sacrificial animals on these altars in order to show their respect and love for him. They also believed that God was going to give them the land of Canaan because he wanted them to rule there and to teach the other nations how to worship him.

Abraham had great trust in God. The patriarch and his people were living happily in the city of Haran when God told them to pack up their possessions on their donkeys and journey into Canaan. Abraham obeyed without question. He did not ask God "Why?" or "How will I get there?" or "What will I do when I get there?" Abraham just obeyed. God loved Abraham because of this. God promised Abraham that his people would become a great nation, the nation of Israel, and that through Abraham all the people of the world would be blessed.

from the
BOOK OF GENESIS
Part 1

The First Day

In the beginning God created the heavens and the earth.
The earth was without form and empty. Darkness was everywhere
and in the darkness the spirit of God moved upon the face of the deep.

GOD SAID: "Let there be light," and there was light.

God saw that it was good and he separated the light from
the darkness. God called the light Day and the darkness
he called Night.

And there were evening and morning: the first day.

The Second Day

GOD SAID: "Let there be a sky in the midst of the waters and let it divide the waters from the waters." Then God made the sky and he separated the waters above from the waters below.

God called the sky Heaven. And there were evening and morning: the second day.

The Third Day

GOD SAID: "Let the waters under the heaven be gathered together in one place, and let the dry land appear." And it was so. God called the dry land Earth, and the waters he called Seas. And he said:

"Let the earth bring forth grass, and yield plants bearing seed, and trees bearing fruit." The earth did so and God saw that it was good.

This was the third day.

The Fourth Day

GOD SAID: "Let there be lights in the sky of heaven to divide the day from the night. Let them be for signs and for seasons, for days and for years. Let them be for lights in the sky of heaven to give light upon the earth."

And it was so.

God made two great lights, the greater light to rule the day, and the lesser light to rule the night. He also made the stars and set them in the sky of heaven to give light upon the earth, to rule over the day and over the night, and to divide the light from the darkness. God saw that it was good.

This was the fourth day.

The Fifth Day

GOD SAID: "Let the waters bring forth in great numbers moving creatures that have life, and let birds fly above the earth in the open sky of heaven."

So God created great whales, and every living creature that moves. These the waters brought forth in great numbers. He created the birds, and saw that all this was good.

He blessed the creatures and said: "Be fruitful and multiply, and fill the waters in the seas. Let the birds also multiply on the earth."

This was the fifth day.

The Sixth Day

GOD SAID: "Let the earth bring forth creatures of all kinds, cattle and creeping things and beasts of the earth." The earth did so and God saw that this was good.

"Let us make man in our image, after our likeness, and let him have power over the fish of the sea and the birds of the air, over the cattle, over all the earth and over everything that moves on the earth."

So God created man in his own image. In the image of God he created man and woman. Male and female created he them. And he blessed them and said to them:

"Be fruitful and multiply. Fill the earth and have power over the fish of the sea and over the birds of the air, over every living thing that moves upon the earth.

"Behold, I have given you every plant bearing seed and every tree yielding fruit which is upon the face of the earth. They shall be your food. To every beast of the earth, to every bird of the air, to everything that creeps upon the earth and has life, I have given the grass and the plants for food." And it was so. God saw everything that he had made, and it was very good.

This was the sixth day.

The Seventh Day

The heavens and the earth were finished and filled with life.
On the seventh day God rested from his work and all that he
had made. God blessed the seventh day and made it a holy day,
because on that day he had rested.

This is how the Lord God made the earth and the heavens,
and every plant before it was in the earth, and every tree
of the field before it grew. And when God had made man, a mist
had gone up from the earth, and had watered the whole surface
of the ground. The Lord God had formed man of the dust
of the ground, and had breathed into him the breath of life,
and man had become a living soul.

THE GARDEN
OF
EDEN

GOD planted a garden in the east, in Eden, and there he put the man whom he had formed. Out of the ground the Lord made trees of every kind to grow, both those that are pleasant to the eye and those that are good for food. In the middle of the garden he planted the tree of life, and the tree of knowledge of good and evil.

A river flowed out of Eden to water the garden, and beneath the garden the river divided and became four rivers. The first was called Pison; the name of the second was Gihon, the third Hiddekel, and the fourth Euphrates.

God took the man and put him into the garden of Eden to care for it and keep it. And God commanded the man, saying:

"Of every tree in the garden you may eat freely, except for the tree of knowledge of good and evil. Of this, do not eat, for in the day that you eat of it, you shall surely die."

Then the Lord God said:

"It is not good that the man should be alone. I will make a companion for him."

But first God brought every beast of the field and every bird of the air, which he had made out of the earth, to

man, to see what he would call them, and what man called each creature, this became that creature's name. Man gave names to the cattle, to the birds of the air, and to every beast of the field. But for himself, man did not find a companion.

So God put man into a deep sleep and as he slept, God took one of his ribs. This rib the Lord God made into woman, and he brought her to man, who said:

"This is now bone of my bones and flesh of my flesh. Her name shall be Woman, because she is taken out of Man." And the man and the woman were naked but they were not ashamed.

THE SERPENT IN THE GARDEN

HE most cunning of the beasts which the Lord had made was the serpent, and the serpent said to the woman: "Did God forbid you to eat the fruit of the trees of the garden?"

The woman said: "We may eat the fruit of the trees of the garden, except the tree which is in the middle of the garden.

"Of this God said, 'You shall not eat of it nor touch it, lest you die.'"

"You will not die," said the serpent. "God knows that the day you eat of the fruit your eyes shall be opened and you will be like gods, knowing good from evil."

The woman looked at the tree and saw that it was pleasant to the eye and good for food. She felt it was to be desired because it would make one wise.

So she picked some of the fruit and ate it, and she gave some also to her husband who was with her, and he ate it.

Then the eyes of both of them were opened, and they knew that they were naked. So they sewed fig leaves together to cover themselves.

In the cool of the day the Lord walked in the garden. The man and the woman heard the voice of the Lord and hid themselves from his presence, among the trees of the garden.

The Lord God called to man saying: "Where are you?"

"I have heard your voice in the garden," said man. "I was afraid, because I was naked, and I hid myself."

"Who told you that you were naked?" asked the Lord God. "Have you eaten the fruit of the tree from which I commanded you not to eat?"

Man said: "The woman whom you gave me to be with me, gave me fruit of the tree and I did eat."

The Lord God said to the woman: "What is this you have done?"

"The serpent tempted me," said the woman, "and I ate."

THEY ARE DRIVEN FROM THE GARDEN

The Lord God said to the serpent:
"Because you have done this, you are cursed above all cattle and above every beast of the field. You shall crawl on your belly and eat dust all the days of your life. I shall make the woman your enemy and her children the enemies of your children.

They shall wound you in the head and you shall wound them in the heel."

To the woman he said:

"I will multiply your suffering. You shall bring forth your children in sorrow and for happiness you shall depend on your husband, and he shall rule over you."

To the man he said: "Because you listened to the voice of your wife and ate of the forbidden fruit, the ground shall be cursed beneath you. In sorrow

you shall eat of it every day of your life. Thorns and thistles it will bring forth for you, and you shall eat the grass of the field. By the sweat of your brow you will earn your bread until you return to the earth, for out of the earth you were taken: dust you are and to dust you shall return."

The Lord God then made coats of skin for the man and his wife, and clothed them.

And the Lord God said:

"Behold, the man is like one of us now, knowing all things. If he were to put out his hand and eat also of the tree of life, he would live forever."

Therefore the Lord God sent man out of the garden of Eden, to till the ground from which he was made. He drove him out, and placed cherubim to the east of the garden of Eden, and a flaming sword which turned in every direction to guard the path to the tree of life.

CAIN AND ABEL, SONS OF ADAM

ADAM named his wife Eve, and she became the mother of all who lived. She gave birth to Cain and said: "The Lord has given me a boy." Then she gave birth to Abel.

Abel became a keeper of sheep and Cain became a tiller of the ground. One day it came to pass that Cain brought some of his harvest as an offering to the Lord, while Abel brought the fattest and choicest of his lambs. The Lord was pleased with Abel and his offering but with Cain and his offering he was not content. Cain was angry and his face fell.

And God said to him:

"Cain, why are you angry? Why are you crestfallen?"

Cain made no answer but later when they were in the fields together, he rose up against his brother and killed him.

And God said to Cain: "Where is Abel your brother?"

"I do not know," said Cain. "Am I my brother's keeper?"

"What have you done?" said God. "The voice of your brother's blood cries out to me from the ground. The earth itself which has received your brother's blood from your hand, now cries out against you. You shall be cursed and from now on, whenever you till the ground, it will not yield its strength to you. A fugitive and a vagabond you shall be on the earth."

"My punishment is more than I can bear," said Cain to the Lord. "Behold, you have driven me out this day from the face of the earth, and from your face I shall hide. I shall be a fugitive and a vagabond on earth, and whoever finds me shall slay me."

"But on whomever kills Cain," said God, "revenge shall be taken seven times over."

And the Lord set a mark upon Cain, so that anyone finding him would not kill him.

After that, Cain went out from the presence of the Lord, and dwelt in the land of Nod, to the east of Eden.

And later in the land of Nod, Cain took a wife and she gave birth to a son who was named Enoch. And Cain built a city and named it after Enoch. From Enoch are descended those who have tents and cattle and those who play upon the harp and the pipe.

Meanwhile Eve gave birth to another son. She called him Seth, for God had given him to her in place of Abel. And in Seth God blessed Adam with a son who resembled his father. Adam lived to a very great age and Eve bore many more sons and daughters.

Thus men began to multiply on the face of the earth and many generations were descended from Adam and Eve. And in the ninth generation there was a descendant named Noah. Noah was a just man, the best of all the men of his time, and he lived by God's rules. He had three sons, named Shem, Ham and Japheth.

NOAH AND THE ARK

"You shall do this because I shall bring upon the earth a great flood which shall destroy every living thing. But with you I will make a promise and the promise shall be called a covenant. You shall enter the ark with your sons, and your wife, and your sons' wives with you.

"Of every living creature upon the earth you shall bring into the ark two of each sort to keep them alive with you. They shall be male and female. Birds of all kinds, cattle and every creeping thing, two of every animal in creation shall come to you for you to keep them alive.

"And take with you some of every kind of food that is eaten. Gather it up, and it shall be food for you and the creatures that are with you."

THE Lord saw that men had become very wicked and that in their minds and their hearts there was only evil. He regretted that he had made man on earth and in his heart he grieved very deeply.

And God said to Noah:

"The end of all flesh is before me. I will destroy all living things on earth for because of them the earth is filled with evil and violence.

"Make an ark of cypress wood," commanded the Lord. "Make rooms in the ark, and cover it inside and out with pitch. Make it in this fashion: the length of the ark shall be four hundred and fifty feet, the breadth of it seventy-five feet, and the height forty-five feet. You shall put a window in it and in its side you shall put a door. The ark shall have three decks: a lower, a second and a third.

THE GREAT FLOOD

Noah had lived to a very great age when the flood of waters came upon the earth.

And God said to Noah:

"Come into the ark, you and all who are with you. Seven days from now, I will cause it to rain upon the earth for forty days and forty nights. And every living thing I have made, I will destroy from off the face of the earth." And Noah did all that the Lord had commanded him.

He entered the ark with Shem and Ham and Japheth, his sons, his own wife and the wives of his sons. Birds and beasts and creeping things of every kind came to Noah and went into the ark, two by two, the male and the female, as God had commanded.

Then the Lord shut Noah in the ark, and the waters of the flood were upon the earth. All the fountains of the great deep were broken up and

the windows of heaven opened. The rain fell upon the earth forty days and forty nights. The waters swelled and lifted the ark above the earth.

The flood spread and the waters continued to rise upon the earth. And the ark floated upon the face of the water. The waters rose higher and higher upon the earth until all the high mountains under heaven were covered. Forty-five feet more did the waters rise above the high mountains and they were indeed covered.

Every living thing that moved upon the earth died: birds, cattle, beasts, every creeping thing that creeps upon the earth, and every man. All in whose nostrils was the breath of life, every man and every living thing which was upon the face of the ground were destroyed. Only Noah and those who were with him remained alive.

God remembered Noah and every living creature with him in the ark. God caused a wind to pass over the earth and to quiet the waters.

THE ARK COMES TO REST

The fountains of the deep and the windows of heaven were stopped and the rain from heaven was restrained. The waters receded for a hundred and fifty days so that in the seven month on the seventeenth day of the month, the ark rested on the mount of Ararat. And the waters continued to decrease until the first day of the tenth month when the peaks of the mountains were seen.

At the end of forty days Noah opened the window of the ark and sent out a raven, which flew to and fro. He also sent out a dove to see if the waters had dried from the ground anywhere. The dove found no rest for the sole of her foot, and she returned to the ark, for the waters still covered

the earth. So Noah put out his hand and took her back into the ark.

He waited seven more days and once again he sent out the dove. The dove came back to him in the evening and, when she did so, there was in her mouth a freshly plucked olive leaf. So Noah knew that the waters had receded from the face of the earth.

Noah waited still another seven days before he sent out the dove. This time the dove did not return.

The water had dried from the earth, so Noah opened the window of the ark. He looked out and saw that the ground was dry.

God spoke to Noah, saying:

"Take with you the birds, the cattle, and every living thing that is with you, that they may breed and raise their young and multiply upon the earth."

So Noah went out, and his sons and his wife and his sons' wives with him. Every beast, every creeping thing and every bird went out of the ark.

And Noah built an altar to the Lord and offered him burnt offerings of every clean beast and every clean fowl.

The Lord smelled the sweet odor and said in his heart:

"I will not curse the ground any more for man's sake. Nor will I ever again strike down every living thing as I have done. As long as the earth remains, seedtime and harvest, cold and heat, summer and winter, day and night will never cease."

God blessed Noah and his sons and said to them:

"Be fruitful and multiply, and replenish the earth. The fear and the dread of you shall be upon every beast of the earth and upon every bird of the air, upon all that moves on the earth and upon all the fishes of the sea. Every moving thing that lives shall be food for you. As once I gave you the green plants, now have I given you all these things."

And God continued, saying:

"Behold, I make my promise to you, and to your children after you, and to every living creature that is with you, and to every living beast of the earth. To the birds and the cattle and all who come out of the ark, I promise that never again will all flesh be cut off by the waters of a flood, nor will a flood destroy the earth.

"This promise is a covenant which I make between myself and you and every creature that is with you, throughout all generations without end.

THE RAINBOW

"I set my rainbow in the cloud and this rainbow shall be a token of the covenant between me and the earth.

"And it shall come to pass when I bring a cloud over the earth, that the rainbow shall be seen in the cloud. I will look upon it, and I will remember the everlasting covenant between me and you and every living creature upon the earth."

And Noah lived a long time after the flood and was a very old man when he died.

Sons were born unto the sons of Noah after the flood, and they went forth and were the fathers of the nations of the earth.

THE TOWER OF BABEL

AFTER God made the covenant with Noah, Noah's descendants increased greatly and one generation succeeded another.

People at this time the earth over were of one language and one speech. And as men journeyed eastwards, they entered a plain in the land of Shinar, where they settled. They said to one another:

"Come, let us make bricks and bake them thoroughly." They used bricks for stone and they had slime for mortar.

And they said: "Let us build a city, and a tower whose top may reach up to heaven. Let us make a name for ourselves lest we be scattered abroad upon the face of the whole earth."

God came down to see the city and the tower which the children of men were building, and said:

"The people of the earth are one people and have only one language. If they begin to do this, nothing will restrain them from doing whatever they conceive. Let us go down, therefore, and confuse their language so that they may not understand one another's speech."

So God scattered them abroad upon the face of the earth, and they left off building the city. And the name of the place is Babel, for there it was that the Lord made a confusion of the language of the earth, and it was in this manner that the Lord scattered the people over the face of the earth.

GOD'S PROMISE TO ABRAM

IN the land of Haran, there lived a man called Abram. Abram was the son of Terah who was descended from Shem. Terah and his family had returned to Haran after living in Ur, when one day God said to Abram:

"Leave your country, and your kinfolk, and your father's house, and go to a land that I will show you. I will make of you a great nation, and I will bless you and make your name great. I will bless those who bless you, and curse those who curse you, and through you all the families of the earth shall be blessed."

So Abram heeded what the Lord had said and departed; he was seventy-five years old when he left Haran. With him he took Sarai his wife, and Lot his brother's son, and all their goods and cattle, and the people they had gathered in Haran. And they went into the land of Canaan.

And they passed through Canaan to Shechem in the plain of Moreh which was occupied then by the Canaanites. At Shechem God appeared to Abram and said:

"This land I will give to your people."

And Abram built an altar to the Lord at Shechem. Then Abram moved and came to a mountain to the east of Bethel where he pitched his tent with Bethel to the west and Ai to the east. Here too he built an altar and called upon the name of the Lord before continuing his journey to the south.

There was famine in the land, so Abram continued to Egypt and lived there until the famine was over. Then he returned to the place between Bethel and Ai where he had built an altar and there he again called on the name of the Lord.

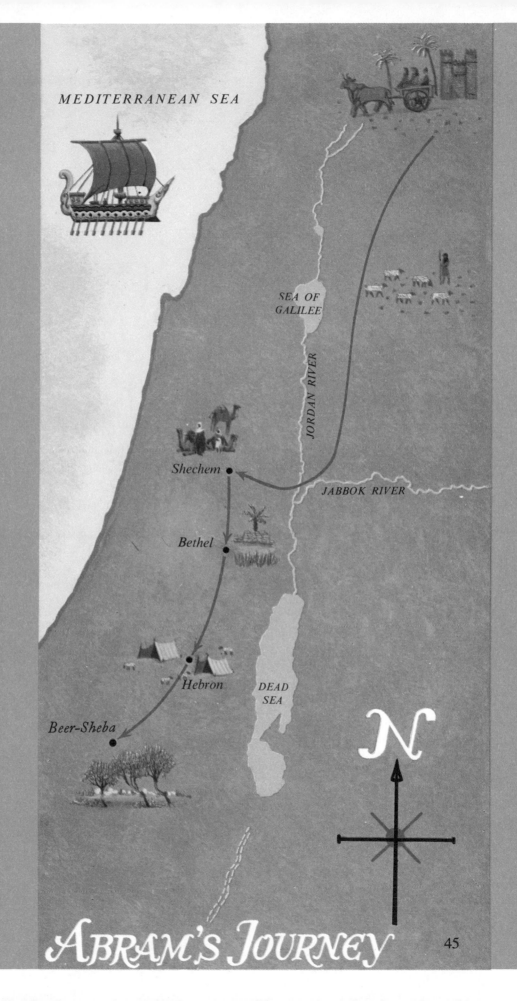

MEDITERRANEAN SEA

SEA OF
GALILEE

JORDAN RIVER

JABBOK RIVER

Shechem

Bethel

Hebron

DEAD
SEA

Beer-Sheba

N

ABRAM'S JOURNEY

ABRAM
AND
LOT

and they separated one from the other.

Abram lived in the land of Canaan and Lot lived in the cities of the plain and pitched his tent near Sodom.

And when Lot had departed, God said to Abram:

"Lift up your eyes now, and look northward, southward, eastward and westward. For all the land which you

BRAM was very rich in cattle, in silver and in gold, and Lot who traveled with him was also very rich, having flocks and herds and tents. The land was not able to support them all; they could not live together in one place and there was trouble between the herdsmen of Abram and the herdsmen of Lot. There were Canaanites and Perizzites also living off the land, so Abram said to Lot:

"Let there be no trouble between you and me, nor between your men and my men, for we are relatives. Is not the whole land before you? Separate yourself, I beg you, from me. If you choose the left hand, I will go to the right. Or if you move to the right then I will go to the left."

Lot lifted his eyes and looked out over the whole plain of Jordan, and saw how well the land was watered everywhere. It was like the garden of the Lord and like parts of the land of Egypt.

So Lot chose for himself all the plain of Jordan. He went toward the east,

see I will give to you and to your descendants forever. And I will make your descendants as the dust of the earth, so that if anybody could count the dust of the earth, he would also be able to count your descendants.

"Arise, walk through the land, the length of it and the breadth of it, for to you I will give it all."

Then Abram moved his tent and went and dwelt in the plain of Mamre which is in Hebron, and there he built an altar to the Lord.

Soon afterward, there was war in the land and Lot and his possessions were captured and taken from Sodom. Abram rescued Lot and his goods and his people, and restored them.

ABRAM'S VISION

FTER these things the word of God came to Abram in a vision, saying:

"Fear not, Abram, I am your shield and your great reward."

"Lord God," Abram said, "what will you give me since I am without children and my heir is a servant, Eliezer of Damascus?"

Then the word of God came to him, saying:

"Not a servant but a child of your own shall be your heir."

He took Abram into the open and said:

"Look now toward heaven, and count the stars if you can do so. As numerous as the stars shall your children and your children's children be." And Abram believed in the Lord and the Lord regarded him with favor.

Then God said to him:

"I am the Lord that brought you out of Ur of the Chaldees, to give you this land to inherit."

"Lord God," Abram said, "how shall I know that I shall inherit it?"

"Bring me a heifer three years old," God said to him, "a she-goat three years old, a ram three years old, a turtle-dove and a young pigeon."

Abram gathered all these animals as offerings. He took them to God and divided them into pieces, laying one against another. But the smallest he did not divide. When the birds of prey came down upon the remains of the offerings Abram drove them away.

As the sun was going down, a deep sleep fell upon Abram and, lo, a great and fearful darkness fell upon him. Then God said to him:

"Know for certain that your children shall be strangers in a land that is not theirs. They shall live in bondage and be oppressed for four hundred years.

"To your children and to all your children's children, I have given this land, from the river of Egypt to the Great River, the river Euphrates. All the people who dwell within it, I have delivered to you."

ABRAHAM IS NAMED

When Abram was ninety-nine years old, the Lord appeared to him and said:

"I am the Almighty God. Walk in my ways and be perfect. I will make my covenant with you, and your people shall increase greatly."

Abram knelt down, his face to the ground, and God talked to him, saying:

"My covenant I shall keep with you. No longer will you be called Abram; from you shall many be descended. Your name shall be Abraham for I have made you a father of many nations. I will keep my covenant with you and my covenant shall be everlasting with you and your descendants through all generations. Your line shall prosper and from it shall arise nations and kings. To you and to them I will give the land of Canaan, in which you are a stranger, as an everlasting possession, and I will be their God.

"As for Sarai, your wife, you shall call her no longer Sarai, but her name shall be Sarah. I will bless her, and from her you shall have a son. She shall be a mother of nations and of kings."

Abraham bowed down and laughed to himself, saying:

"Can a man a hundred years old have a son? And Sarah, a woman of ninety, can she have a child?"

Then God said:

"Sarah, your wife, shall bear a son, and you will call him by the name Isaac. With him and with his children after him will I make my everlasting covenant."

But the nation that shall oppress them I will judge, and afterwards they shall emerge with great possessions.

"You yourself shall go to your fathers in peace, and be buried in a good old age. Your children shall return here in the fourth generation."

When the sun was down and it was dark, behold, a smoking furnace and a burning lamp passed between the pieces of the offering.

And on that day God made a covenant with Abram, saying:

THE THREE ANGELS

And it came to pass that when Abraham was sitting in the door of his tent in the plains of Mamre, the Lord appeared to him in the form of three angels in the heat of the day. Abraham raised his eyes and saw three men standing before him. He ran to meet them and bowed to the ground, saying:

"My Lords, if I have now found favor in your sight, do not pass away, I beg you, from your servant. Let a little water be fetched and wash your feet and rest yourselves under the tree. I will bring bread to refresh you. Comfort your hearts, then you may go on your way."

They said to him: "Do as you have said." So Abraham hastened into the tent where Sarah his wife was and said:

"Quickly, make three measures of fine meal, knead it, and bake cakes upon the hearth."

Then he ran to the herd and fetched a good and tender calf, and

gave it to a young man to prepare.

Abraham then took butter and milk, and the calf, and set the food before the men. He stood by them under the tree while they ate.

"Where is Sarah, your wife?" they asked him.

"There, in her tent," he said.

And one of the men said, "Sarah your wife shall have a son."

Sarah, standing in the tent doorway behind him, heard this. She and Abraham were old and they were beyond the time for having children.

Sarah therefore laughed to herself.

Then God said to Abraham:

"Why did Sarah laugh, saying she is too old to have a child? Is there anything the Lord cannot do? At the appointed time, Sarah shall have a son."

Sarah denied that she had laughed, for she was afraid. But God said:

"No, you did laugh."

The Lord did as he had promised, and Sarah bore Abraham a son in his old age at the time chosen by God, and Abraham called the son Isaac, a name which means 'He will laugh.'

A WIFE
FOR
ISAAC

ANY years later, Abraham was very old and the Lord had blessed him in all things. One day Abraham said to the eldest servant of his house, who managed all that he had:

"Give me your hand, I pray you. I will make you swear by the Lord, the God of heaven and the God of earth, that you will not choose a wife for my son from the daughters of the Canaanites, among whom I dwell. But you will go to my country and there among my own people you will choose a wife for my son Isaac."

"What if the woman that is chosen will not be willing to follow me to this land?" said the servant. "Must I take your son back again to the land from which you came?"

Abraham said to him: "Beware, above all, that you do not take my son there again. The Lord God of heaven, who took me from my father's house and from the land of my people, made a covenant with me, and said to me: 'To your children will I give this land.'

"He shall send his angel before you, and you shall choose there a wife for my son. If the woman does not willingly follow you, then you shall be freed from your oath. Only do not take my son to that land."

So the servant gave his hand to Abraham, his master, and swore to do as he had been told.

ABRAHAM'S SERVANT DEPARTS

Then the servant took ten of his master's camels, for all the goods of his master were in his care, and he departed.

He went to Mesopotamia to the

city of Nahor. There he made his
camels kneel down outside the city,
beside a well of water, at the time of
the evening when the women went out
to draw water.

Then he prayed:

"O Lord, God of my master Abraham, I beg of you, send me good
fortune today, and show kindness to
my master, Abraham. Behold, I stand
here by the spring, and the daughters
of the men of the city are coming to
draw water. Let it come to pass that
the girl to whom I shall say: 'Let down
your pitcher, so that I may drink,' and

who will say to me: 'Drink! And I
will give your camels a drink also,' let
this girl be the wife you have chosen
for your servant Isaac. By this I shall
know that you have shown kindness to
my master."

Before he had finished speaking
a young girl appeared. She was Rebekah, whose father was the son of
Nahor, Abraham's brother. She carried her pitcher upon her shoulder. The
girl was very fair to look upon, young
and unmarried.

She went down to the well, filled her
pitcher, and came up.

REBEKAH AT THE WELL

Abraham's servant ran to meet her and said: "Let me drink a little water from your pitcher."

And she said: "Drink, my lord."

Then she quickly lowered the pitcher upon her hand and gave him a drink. When she had finished giving him a drink, she said: "I will draw water for your camels also, until they have finished drinking."

She hurried and emptied her pitcher into the trough, ran to the well to draw water, and drew it for all his camels. The man held his peace, wondering whether the Lord had made his journey successful or not.

As the camels had finished drinking, he took out a golden ear-ring of half a shekel weight and two bracelets for her hands, also of heavy gold. "Whose daughter are you?" he asked. "Tell me, I beg of you. Is there room in your father's house for me to spend the night?"

She said to him: "I am the daughter of Bethuel, the son of Milcah and Nahor. Of both straw and food we have enough, and also room to lodge in."

Then the man bowed down his head and worshiped the Lord, saying, "Blessed be the Lord, God of my master Abraham, who has not kept his mercy and his truth from my master. The Lord led me on the way to the house of my master's brother."

The girl ran on to her mother's house, and told these things.

LABAN, REBEKAH'S BROTHER

Now Rebekah had a brother, and his name was Laban. When he saw the ear-rings and the bracelets upon his sister's hands, and when he heard the words of Rebekah his sister, Laban ran out and found the servant of Abraham standing by the camels at the well.

Laban said:

"Come in, you whom the Lord has blessed. Why do you stand outside? For I have prepared the house, and there is room for the camels."

So the man came into the house, and Laban unharnessed the camels and gave them straw and feed. He brought water to wash the man's feet and the feet of the men who were with him.

They set meat before the man to eat, but he said: "I will not eat until I have told my errand."

"Speak on," said Laban.

The man said: "I am Abraham's servant. The Lord has blessed my master greatly, and he has become great. The Lord has given him flocks and herds, silver and gold, menservants and maidservants, camels and asses. And Sarah, my master's wife, bore a son to my master when she was old, and to him he has given all that he has."

Then the servant told how Abraham had sent him to find a wife for Isaac, and how the Lord had led him to Rebekah. "And now if you will deal kindly and truly with my master, tell me. If not, tell me also, so that I may know which way to turn."

Then Laban and Bethuel answered and said: "All this comes from the Lord. We cannot say anything to you, bad or good. Behold, Rebekah is here before you; take her and go. Let her be your master's son's wife, as the Lord has said."

When Abraham's servant heard their words, he worshiped the Lord, bowing himself to the earth. And he brought out jewels of silver and jewels of gold and clothing, and gave them to Rebekah. To her brother and her mother he also gave precious things.

They ate and drank, he and the men that were with him. They spent the night and rose up in the morning. Then he said: "Send me back to my master."

Rebekah's brother and her mother said: "Let the girl remain with us a few days, at least ten. After that she shall go with you."

"Do not hinder me," he said to them. "The Lord has made my errand successful. Send me away, that I may go to my master." "We will call the girl and ask her," they said.

They called Rebekah and said to her: "Will you go with this man?"

"I will go," she said.

So they sent away Rebekah their sister, and her nurse, and Abraham's servant, and his men. They blessed Rebekah, and Rebekah arose with her maidens, and they rode upon the camels and followed the man. And the servant took Rebekah and went his way.

ISAAC AND REBEKAH

Isaac went out of his dwelling in the south country to walk in the field, at the end of the day. He lifted his eyes and, behold, he saw the camels were coming.

Rebekah lifted her eyes and saw Isaac. She lighted from her camel and said to the servant: "Who is this man walking in the field toward us?"

"It is my master's son," said the servant.

Thereupon, she took a veil and covered herself. The servant told Isaac everything he had done. Then Isaac brought her into the tent of Sarah, his mother. Rebekah became his wife, and he loved her.

ILLUSTRATED GLOSSARY

Canaan (p. 46)

The area along the eastern shore of what is now the Mediterranean Sea, but which was known in biblical times as the Great Sea, was the land of Canaan. Canaan was God's promised land.

The Canaan of ancient times was made up of the area that we now know as Israel, Lebanon, and part of Jordan. Later, the part of Canaan between the towns of Dan and Beersheba, where the Israelites lived, became known as Palestine.

Canaanites (p. 46)

The people who carried the name of Canaan (grandson of Noah and son of Ham) were called the Canaanites. They were related to the Hebrews. In Canaan, the Canaanites built fine cities, and around each one they put up a wall to keep out invaders. Outside the walls, the people tended their farms. Each Canaanite city had its own king.

The Canaanites gave their name to the land of Canaan, which God promised to Abraham and his family. Much later, the land of Canaan was invaded by the Israelites, who captured most of the cities.

Cattle (p. 44)

To us, the word cattle usually means cows, bulls, and oxen. But the cattle that Abraham owned were, for the most part, goats and sheep. These animals made up most of the wandering Hebrews' wealth. The hair of sheep and goats was used for making cloth for tents, sackcloth, and clothing. Goat's milk was an especially important food for drinking and for cheese-making. The animals' meat, especially that of kids and young lambs, was prized by the Hebrews.

Chaldees (p. 48)

The Semitic people who ruled in the city of Ur at the time of the Babylonian Empire were called Chaldees, or Chaldeans. The city was often called "Ur of the Chaldees."

Covenant (p. 41)

The Hebrews called a promise between two people a covenant. In a covenant a strong person usually promised to take care of a weak one. In return, the weaker one promised to do something for the stronger.

God made a covenant with Abraham and the other patriarchs, Isaac and Jacob. To Abraham he said: "Leave your country and go to a land I will show you. I will make of you a great nation."

To Isaac, Abraham's son, the Lord said: "I am with you. I will bless you and give you many descendents."

When Jacob, Isaac's son, was fleeing from Canaan, the Lord said to him: "I will give this land to you and your descendents. I will take care of you wherever you go, and I will bring you back to this land."

In return for his goodness to the Hebrews, God expected them to live as he wished and to be loyal to him. That was their part of the covenant.

Fig leaves (p. 31)

Adam and Eve covered themselves with leaves from the fig tree. These leaves are large and thick enough to be sewn together. Fig trees produce delicious sweet fruit and are common trees in the Mideast even today.

Perizzites (p. 46)

The Perizzites were a small tribe that lived in the land of Canaan.

River of Egypt (p. 49)

The River of Egypt is a small stream that begins in the wilderness in the northern part of Sinai. It flows northeast to empty into the Mediterranean Sea, or Great Sea as it was called in biblical times. This tiny stream was quite important because it was a border of the Promised Land.

Shem (Semite) (p. 38)

One of Noah's sons was named Shem. In Genesis he is described as the father of several tribes whose people then became known as the children of Shem, or Semites. Semites, or Semitic people, speak languages that are very much alike. The best-known Semites in today's world are the Jewish people and the Arabs.

Shinar, Land of (p. 42)

The rich plain between the common mouth of the Tigris and the Euphrates rivers was called the land of Shinar. Early in history, Shinar was settled by the Sumerians, who were not Semites. They occupied the land about 200 miles from where the rivers flow into the Persian Gulf.

Sodom (p. 46)

A city that was once located at the southern end of the Dead (Salt) Sea,

Sodom was known for its people's evil ways. It is believed that Sodom, together with Gomorrah, another wicked city, sank below the waters of the Dead Sea.

Thorns and thistles (p. 33)

Thorns and thistles are wild plants seen mostly in dry and desert areas. They are covered with sharp spines. When God said to Adam and Eve, "Thorns and thistles will the earth bring forth for you," he meant that they would have to work to grow food, because all the earth would offer would be wild thorns and thistles.

The Tree of Knowledge (p. 26)

The Bible does not tell us what kind of fruit tree the Tree of Knowledge was. It is commonly believed that the forbidden fruit was an apple, but apples do not grow in the land of the Bible. Some scholars believe the fruit was the pomegranate, from a tree that is common in Bible lands.

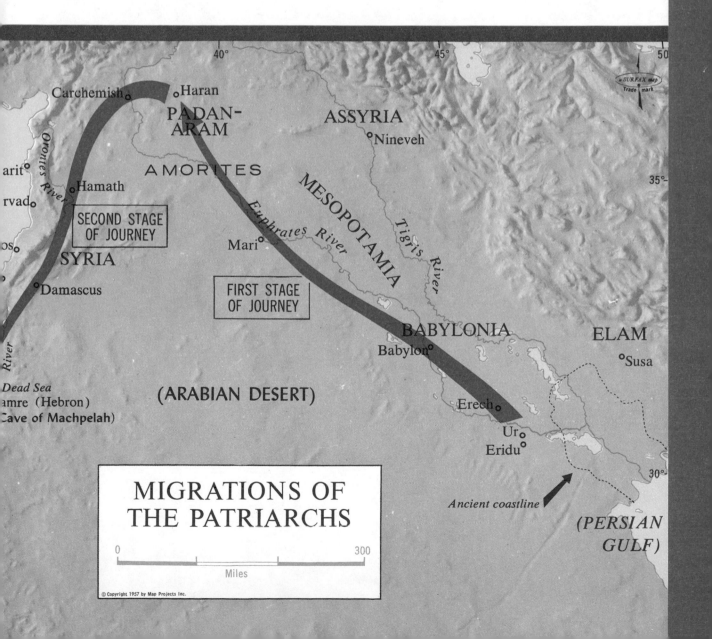

MIGRATIONS OF THE PATRIARCHS

0   300

Miles

© Copyright 1957 by Map Projects Inc.